The Storage Book

The Storage Book

Over 250 ideas for stylish home storage

Cynthia Inions

ABBEVILLE PRESS PUBLISHERS

NEW YORK LONDON PARIS

First published in the United States of America in 1997
by Abbeville Press, 488 Madison Avenue, New York, NY 10022

First published in Great Britain in 1997
by Mitchell Beazley, an imprint of Reed Consumer Books Limited
Michelin House, 81 Fulham Road,
London SW3 6RB
and Auckland, Melbourne, Singapore and Toronto

First edition
2 4 6 8 10 9 7 5 3 1

ISBN 0-7892-0400-2

The publishers have made every effort to ensure that all instructions given in this
book are accurate and safe but they cannot accept liability for any resulting injury,
damage, or loss to either person or property, whether direct or consequential and
howsoever arising.

contents

introduction

below Inexpensive clear and opaque plastic products in plain and simple style offer multiple storage solutions in living areas, garages, and workshops. (Unit from Muji.)

left Reuse industrial or office furniture and fixtures as practical storage items. A clothing locker from a public swimming pool is given new status as a key storage item in a New York studio apartment.

below Modern manufacturers constantly rework traditional storage concepts such as roll-top desks or decorative armoires in keeping with multifunctional homes. (Carlo Madera bureau.)

left An inventive alternative to traditional jars for storing herbs and spices, this is a simple combination of a plastic bag and an airtight clip – keeping its contents fresh. Hang multiple bags in a horizontal line.

above Combine modern, state-of-the-art design with basic practicality in singular storage items like this impressive Stanley cupboard. (Manufactured by Dialogica.)

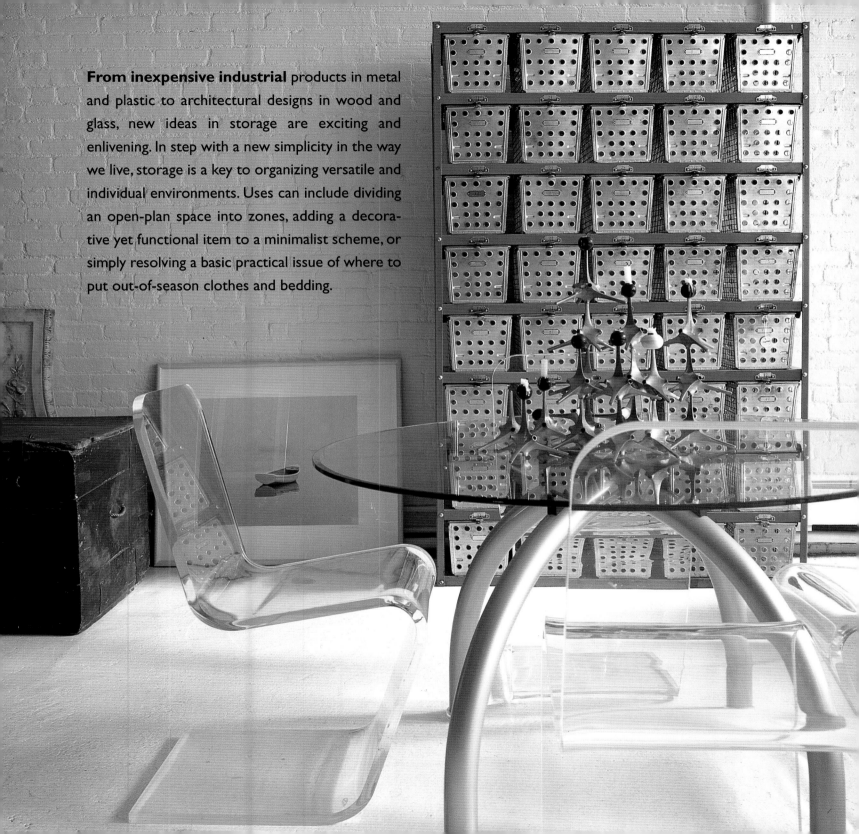

From inexpensive industrial products in metal and plastic to architectural designs in wood and glass, new ideas in storage are exciting and enlivening. In step with a new simplicity in the way we live, storage is a key to organizing versatile and individual environments. Uses can include dividing an open-plan space into zones, adding a decorative yet functional item to a minimalist scheme, or simply resolving a basic practical issue of where to put out-of-season clothes and bedding.

Of the many inspirational and practical storage solutions to revolutionize kitchens, liberate bedrooms, and transform living space, some will meet your current requirements exactly, while others will need a little modification to fit in perfectly.

Some schemes will suggest a whole new way to live. Perhaps it is time to review and reorganize your domestic environment. Yet before investing in new storage or a structural redesign, begin with a critical edit of everything you possess, from kitchen utensils, clothing, books, and electrical equipment to furniture and fixtures and fittings.

Simplicity, freedom, and a sense of space are not about finding a place to store every single thing. They are about identifying what is essential, functional, and inspirational, keeping these elements and giving away, selling, or recycling everything else. Consider efficient industrial shelving when planning kitchens; simplify living space with modular storage cabinets for everything from tableware to CD players and books; or screen all your clothes and bed linen behind translucent sliding glass panels in bedrooms.

Of the many inspirational ideas in this book, the majority can fit into your home with ease to solve difficult storage problems.

above Semi-transparent doors or sliding panels signal an exciting direction in storage design, as seen in this cupboard by Maarten Van Severen.

right Dynamic sculptural forms such as this, or artistic storage items in wood, glass, or stone add a welcome organic element to minimalist areas.

left A preference for combining kitchen and dining space places a new emphasis on kitchen planning and design. Opt for an efficient easy-to-maintain system with ample hideaway storage to provide a simple but welcoming environment. (Mediterranea by Arc Linea.)

left New designs like this magazine rack offer fresh thinking on conventional storage. For alternative ad hoc solutions, use filing cabinets for clothing or metal trash cans for laundry to add vitality to everyday storage solutions.

storage with style

period
style

Grand memorials to a different age, period storage pieces can work within a contemporary interior if you adopt a minimalist approach. Unless you favor living in historically faithful surroundings, cut back or pack away ornaments, simplify decoration with plain colors, and install impressive storage items that have a degree of formality and symmetry – ideally, a single expansive piece for every situation. For example, a good-size armoire can provide ample storage for books, china, foodstuffs, clothing, or electronic equipment in just about any setting. A chest of drawers is equally versatile, while colonial-style chests and wicker hampers will provide extra small-scale storage.

left An antique chest of drawers is the main storage item in the library of a New York conversion. It stands formally at one end of the main room to define a writing and reading space. A packing trunk and ethnic baskets store paperwork. (Design: Tricia Foley.)

above Simple log baskets on each side of an imposing stone and carved-wood mantel fulfill an essential fireside storage function. They also make attractive alternatives to the traditional type of ornamental container. (Design: Tricia Foley.)

left Too precious and formal to use for food, an antique silver platter makes an imaginative flatware storage tray. Decorative and practical, it can be transferred easily from kitchen shelf to any table setting.

Simplicity and freedom from clutter was the defining feature of a Shaker dwelling. Shaker homes were havens of orderliness, in tune with strict spiritual beliefs. For believers, living as large communal families and sharing everything, it was essential that even the smallest household item had a place in which everyone would know where to find it, use it, and put it back for the next person. Mother Ann, founder of the Shakers in North America in the 1770s, set out directives for this orderly way of life. Her guidelines were plain common sense: "Provide places for all your things so that you may know where to find them at any time, day or night."

shaker
style

left Peg rails can take on a different use in every room. Thread lengths of rope or leather through shelf tops and loop them over peg rails in kitchens, bathrooms, and halls for small-scale storage.

below These sculptural storage boxes and bowls are as appropriate to a period dwelling as a modern interior. Color-code individual items to identify what is inside.

above Saucepans and shelves for spice jars hang from a peg rail, making them easily accessible for cooking and food preparation. Built-in kitchen cabinets provide a place for everything in a simple arrangement of multisized drawers under an oiled-wood counter.

opposite A peg rail running around a plain wall is a key feature of a Shaker-style interior for storing essential everyday items. Shakers did not believe in display for the sake of it, so if you do not use an item often, do not hang it on a peg rail.

The simplicity and honest functionalism of historic Shaker dwellings, with a delight in space and respect for nature's gifts, is essential inspiration for contemporary interiors. Simple storage along Shaker lines organizes objects according to common sense: each item is given a place appropriate to how often it is used, or to its size and function. Storage furniture can include floor-to-ceiling cabinets and chests of drawers in pine, maple, and cherry wood for storing all kinds of household items from tableware to clothing. Peg rails around every room provide easy-access hanging space for brooms and everyday items, keeping the floor clear and easy to sweep. Freestanding furniture is best kept to a minimum, with only as many chairs as people to sit on them. And when chairs are not in use, store them off the floor on the peg rails. Everything should play a part efficiently and harmoniously — another key Shaker directive that is as relevant now as it was to Mother Ann in the 1770s.

left Shaker ladderback chairs are designed for hanging out of the way on pegs when not in use. Make sure that your peg rail is securely anchored to a wall before you hang any kind of chair in this way.

country
style

above Hanging by a nail on a wall in a utility room, a shallow basket is a useful container for a jumble of pegs and sticks. It exemplifies the practicality of country style.

right A country kitchen flatware tray with a central division neatly frames and separates antique knives and forks for decorative and functional storage.

above Old-fashioned food "safes" with fine wire mesh on wooden frames make useful storage cabinets for china, table linen, and dry food or cans.

right A wooden bucket with individual staves bound in place by a metal hoop is a convenient place to store kitchen utensils and turns everything it contains into a decorative feature.

From pocket-sized cottages to grand houses, or even urban interiors with an identity crisis, the traditions at the heart of country style – mixing, not matching – will apply. This means the freedom to combine inexpensive thrift-store finds, homespun antiques, special pieces that have a family history, and anything you like the look of.

left In this informal New York apartment, decoration is in homespun-style. A ceramic dish overflowing with family photographs and a painted box used to store letters provide personal effects with originality and spirit.

below A French wire basket split into sections provides simple but effective storage for glasses. Stack this type of lightweight container with glasses, bottles of olive oil, and jars of condiments or spices and carry it directly to the table — indoors or out.

right Strong lines on simple furniture are key to the appeal of country-style interiors. This kitchen hutch provides ample storage for all kitchen items, plus additional space to display a collection of antique china.

Adhering to a single period style — or even choosing furniture from one country of origin — will not result in a typically informal country-style mix. To get the look right, start with distinctive basics — for kitchens, perhaps a scrubbed Italian table with a flatware drawer and an English hutch. A less conventional alternative would be to mix an individual shelf unit with a contrasting chest of drawers. For living rooms, look out for European painted food "safes"; these are ideal for storing books and stereo equipment. And decorative Spanish or French armoires provide ample storage in country-style interiors. Visit flea markets and auctions, and consider stripping or painting anything you find there. Keep a set of room measurements with you before you buy.

Once you have decided on your main pieces of country-style storage furniture and installed them, you can add the smaller items: traditional ceramics, decorative metalware, and anything craft-oriented, like handmade boxes. For inexpensive solutions, check out local farmer's markets or super-markets for vegetable boxes or wooden crates—they are perfect for kitchen storage.

In a radical break with traditions in craft and ornamentation, modernist designs from 1910 to the 1950s were influenced by new technology. The bold architectural shapes of modernist pieces, mass produced from industrial plastics, plywood, and steel, still generate a buzz and exert a powerful influence on contemporary designs. Many originals continue to be produced, so it is possible to buy the real thing. Alternatively, collect classics from dealers or markets, track down inexpensive chain-store equivalents, or take inspiration from the colors and simple shapes of these pieces to revamp existing storage items with metal doors, new pulls, and paint.

contemporary
inspiration

below Highly architectural and colorful, Charles Eames's storage cabinet combines form and function. In a living area, such a piece can provide useful storage for electrical equipment and books.

right In this New York galley kitchen, built-in storage cabinets and appliances are installed along one wall. This creates a space for table and chairs. (Architects: Fernlund + Logan.)

left Inspired by mass-produced designs from the 1950s, this horizontal aluminum wall track system with organic-looking brackets provides an architectural support for heavy-duty glass shelving. (Design: Ali Tayar.)

below The Isoken donkey provides compact multi-storage for living room paraphernalia, including magazines, newspapers, and books, in lightweight sculptural plywood.

musica viva

v. einem
schönberg
strawinsky

right Postwar Scandinavian design brings a modernist perspective to a New York apartment. A teak cabinet stores CDs in an open-plan area. (Architects: Solveig Fernlund & Neil Logan.)

left To modernists, metal in design is the equivalent of concrete in architecture – bold and essential. This revamp to replace wood veneer cabinet doors with inexpensive metal gives an ordinary New York kitchen-in-a-corridor a dynamic new look.

left The graphic boxlike dimensions of a 1950s Knoll teak cabinet with painted steel legs is offset by traditional paneling. The glass vases are modern. For modernist storage on a budget, mount square kitchen wall cabinets on the wall at sideboard height and customize them further with paint or a change of pulls.

Storage cabinets in the spirit of modernism have a utilitarian simplicity. Many contemporary geometric or modular designs encompass this industrial style, from boxlike television cabinets to cubic bookcases. Put together a wall of cubes with interchangeable solid and glass doors and create your own modernist version. Leave some cubes open, with or without shelves. A strong geometric frame will overpower the disorder within, so a typical jumble of books and magazines will not look out of place.

Explore the potential of boxlike wall cabinets. Kitchen suppliers usually stock a good selection. Install a row along a hallway, bedroom, or living room at sideboard height with invisible hardware. Place one cabinet in a bathroom for toiletries, or make a square of four in a living room to store books or videos – perhaps paint them different colors, or experiment with one color for the frame and different colors for each door.

Even if your budget does not run to new designs, it is possible to enjoy the poetic plainness of the modern movement. Paint existing cabinets and change pulls to simple metal disks, or replace doors with metal or plastic panels.

Beyond presenting almost limitless storage possibilities, ethnic furniture and folk artifacts from around the world seem to exert a magical spell on the postindustrial dwellers of the Western world. The bright colors of African baskets or the graphic simplicity of a Japanese chest can add a powerfully primitive or exotic presence to a modern interior. The key to incorporating these elements successfully into modern settings is to put them to use as functional everyday items.

ethnic
ideas

left A simple 19th-century temple cupboard in teak from West Rajasthan, India forms part of a collection in David Wainwright's London town house. Set on wooden wheels, it transfers easily to a modern interior.

left In the spirit of a cave dwelling, this hewn stone and wood nightstand exerts a powerful force in a California interior. Along with kitchen cabinets made out of driftwood-effect planks, wicker baskets, and large pots, storage is primitive style.

above Often lacking in modern interiors, decoration is an essential feature of ethnic art. An elaborate artifact or piece of furniture, like this finely carved Nuristani chest offset by a plain backdrop, can be both practical and decorative.

right Textile designer Jack Lenor Larsen brings Japanese aesthetics to a collection of ceramics, sculpture, and paintings in a New York apartment. Set out with precision on glass shelves within a wooden framework, the collection is seen or hidden, thanks to traditional sliding screens.

Inspirational as well as exotic, many ethnic storage ideas originate from ancient cultures and lifestyles and were designed to be portable – for example, stacking and nesting baskets from space-conscious Japan, wooden merchants' chests from spice-trading India, and woven sacks for clothing and cooking pots from the nomadic shepherds of the Atlas mountains.

Still being made today, and using methods and materials little changed for centuries and easily transportable for travelers and tourists, many bold and simple items transfer well to modern-day interiors as essentially practical storage solutions.

With furniture – particularly wooden items such as a Mexican sideboard or Korean trunk – it is a good idea to buy imports from specialist dealers close to home. There is less risk of an infestation of exotic insects and, unless the item was shipped very recently, less chance of climatic shock reaction – such as splitting or cracking wood.

left A majestic antique Japanese *mizuya*, once a silent witness to formal tea ceremonies, in cypress wood provides flexible storage with an array of drawers and sliding panels.

right Hand-woven baskets on open wooden shelves provide decorative and accessible small-scale storage in a New York bedroom. Like a visual index, the pattern, color, and shape of each basket identifies its contents.

above A wall of cabinets in blue are the main feature of this interior. (Courtesy of the Atlanta Historical Society, Inc.)

left Malcolm Temple's ornamental sea chest is crafted from basic building materials. The frame is carved, stained, and varnished composite board and gives an appearance of Oriental wood.

Specialist dealers in ethnic items can provide essential back-up and advice about cleaning, repair, and restoration. For inexpensive small-scale storage solutions — such as baskets, metalware, wooden bowls, and boxes — check out your local shopping mall, craft stores, and craft fairs.

Selecting ethnic storage pieces that are functional as well as decorative is very important. Presenting a Rajasthani temple cupboard as an artistic souvenir will alienate it from its new surroundings; however, put into useful service as a linen or china chest, its relocation will make sense.

Folk art pieces such as Pueblo Indian water jars or punch-pattern tin boxes from New Mexico can all find new identities as decorative yet essentially practical storage items. Aim to be selective, and think about how ethnic colors and organic shapes will fit in with modern-day industrial precision and exactness. For example, a vast handmade terra-cotta grain jar, bargained for with passion in a Moroccan souk, will invariably look quite different on a concrete floor in an urban kitchen. Yet juxtapositions like this can express the power of ethnic design.

hall and porch

hall and
porch

Entrance halls are active transition areas from outside to inside and require effective storage for dropping off or picking up outdoor clothing, a change of footwear, keys, mail, and perhaps a bicycle. Yet entrance halls should also be welcoming spaces – the first space that you and your visitors will see. So it is important to create a practical, friendly space that is free from clutter or an impassable collection of disorderly clothes or equipment. Ideally, keep the area directly inside the front door clear for quick and easy access, and plan any storage solutions to begin beyond the doormat.

left The area behind this sweeping stairway provides storage for cleaning equipment, tools, and out-of-season household items. (Architects: Munkenbeck + Marshall.)

above A photographer's trunk converted to household storage is in keeping with this industrial-style interior. A collection of antique clocks cleverly inhibits a buildup of clutter.

right An open-plan studio becomes a work/living space with the addition of a bed platform, basic stair, and a partition to create an office. A hat stand defines the entrance area.

For clothing, umbrellas, and bags, there is a wide choice of hooks – from minimalist metal buttons to wooden pegs or decorative iron-work – that will fit in with contemporary or traditional environments. A wooden or metal pole spanning an alcove and equipped with a good supply of coat hangers will provide useful hanging space. If space is available and storage requirements exceed a few coat hooks, line hall walls with cabinets or a combination of shelves and hanging rods. Folding doors, sliding panels, and roll-up shades provide space-conscious alternatives to conventional doors.

Within an open-plan environment, consider constructing a simple enclosure to create storage and a sense of division from inner and outer space. A permanent wall or panel, or a less dense glass partition to let light pass through, will provide an essential cut-off from the front door and offer a potential storage area with hooks attached to the wall or a freestanding coat stand or clothes rod.

left A simple sandblasted glass screen conceals a basic clothes rod and contrasts to great effect with a traditional hall table and collection of artifacts. (Architects: Stickland Coombe.)

Hall landings can present welcome and surprising storage possibilities. A bookshelf placed next to a chair and good light can offer a peaceful reading spot. Alternatively a desk, table, or flip-down worktop with shelves for paperwork and files above can provide office or study space. All kinds of cabinets, from armoires to custom-built designs that make the best use of any odd corners, are perfect for over-spill or out-of-season clothing, linen, spare bedding, books, or sports equipment.

Understair cabinets provide useful storage for bulky items like vacuum cleaners, ironing boards, and the usual closet overspill. If there is space, put in a cupboard or shelf for valuable extra storage. If space is really limited, consider the potential for storage above doorways. A shelf across the width of a door frame on bracket supports is useful for books. If you want to conceal a jumble of odds and ends, store them in boxes on the shelf. Consider extending the shelf to run around a landing or along a row of doorways. (Check that this will not create an obstruction before you go ahead.) Alternatively, frame a doorway with narrow shelves from floor to ceiling and create a mini-library.

left A traditional wooden peg rail for coats, and bare floorboards for heavy-duty footwear and walking sticks provide highly functional and down-to-earth storage in this basic mudroom in Stephen Mack's house.

above Narrow tables provide ideal storage for busy hallways, and simple structures like this folding plant table take up less space than formal pieces.

left It is hard to beat a peg rail for practical storage in a hall. Perhaps put two peg rails at different heights in the hallway for adult and children's outdoor clothing.

living room

open and shut
cases

Whether you spend time reading, listening to music, watching television, or relaxing on a sofa with friends, flexible storage solutions are the key to organizing a multifunctional and informal living space. From building-block modular cabinets with open and shut storage to architectural holes in the wall, modern ideas for accommodating diverse recreational interests will contribute to creating an environment that is both practical and personal.

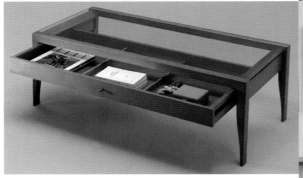

above This pearwood table with a glass top includes a drawer underneath for magazines and books, and space for games, collections, and specialized items. (From Arc Linea.)

above This flexible arrangement of storage building blocks features shelves and divisions. Begin with one square and add on new cabinets to meet requirements. (From Arc Linea.)

left A simple wooden "D" shelf with steel brackets can create a striking display for a selection of art books and personal memorabilia. (Design: Annabelle Selldorf.)

right Simplicity, light, and space are key elements in this New York apartment. A simple early 20th-century French cabinet contrasts with a plain shelf for displaying prints. (Design: Vicente Wolf.)

Storing every possession on view can look chaotic and overpower a living space, yet if everything is hidden away, a room can appear unwelcoming. For a sense of order with a human touch, mix open and shut storage for entertainment equipment as well as displays of selected personal items.

Individual preference is a good guide when planning what to reveal and what to conceal — especially if you have one main leisure activity. For multifunctional spaces, select something of all key interests to be displayed and conceal bulky back-up equipment or specialized collections. Alternatively, use specific storage items, perhaps a cabinet or shelf system, for individual activities and divide a living space into recreational zones.

Store collections of videos, CDs, or books in a set of drawers, a cabinet, or a storage system with sliding front panels. Keep a selection of current favorites on hand in an open rack, single shelf, or simple informal stack.

right This spacious living area contains a mixture of open and shut storage. CDs and videos reside in a set of drawers, while African artifacts are displayed on a simple oak table. (Furniture designer/maker: Andrew Mortada.)

Using open storage to display artifacts, collections, photographs, or anything of personal interest that is visually stimulating enlivens any space. Choose a storage system that is relevant to the items that you intend to display. For example, a bold system of parallel wooden shelves is perfect for displaying modern sculpture or black-and-white photographic prints in a contemporary environment, yet it might overpower a colorful collection of American folk art or Japanese ceramics.

Before opting for a particular storage system – either open shelving or shelves within a framework – check the weight and space requirements of the items. If a collection of artifacts or electronic equipment is complete, opt for permanent shelving with wall brackets or metal supports; or, for invisible mountings, embed metal rods into the wall and then into the back of wooden shelves.

Lay out everything for display on the floor and map out an arrangement or make a storage plan. Double-check measurements with special attention to depth, and leave adequate space front and back, especially for equipment with cables and connections.

left An effective contrast of modernity and antiquity in a New York apartment. A display shelf for photographs is an ideal, flexible storage solution. (Design: Vicente Wolf.)

below In keeping with a graphic modern environment, a wall shelf with invisible hardware presents a clean-cut profile. (Furniture from Arc Linea.)

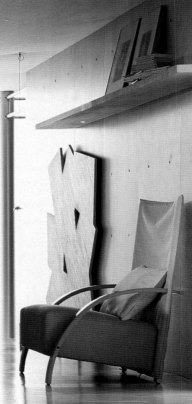

right A collection of cheap and cheerful figures from South America are displayed prominently on this network of glass shelves within a simple wooden framework.

left A strikingly simple wall-mounted shelving system with tracks and adjustable brackets in anodized aluminum is as visually appealing as the ceramics on display. (Ellen's Brackets by Ali Tayar for Parallel Design.)

Some storage options are in fact architectural solutions – structural add-ons or details that appear to be part of the framework of a space. Ambitious ideas, such as replacing partition walls with floor-to-ceiling storage systems accessible from both sides, or adding a parallel wall next to an existing wall to create storage space in between, require forward planning and imagination. For ideas on this scale, consult an architect for creative input and incorporate any suggestions or recommendations at the initial planning or refurbishment stage for maximum economy and minimal disruption.

For minimalists, the appeal of structural storage is to devise a practical framework for living free from the clutter of individual items of furniture, while allowing for possessions. However, be aware that this level of simplicity throws into relief anything on display. Keep visible elements either honest and functional, or sculptural and artistic; perhaps a compact music system, African figure, or Japanese light.

right A desk and video shelf, suspended between a sculptural plaster wall and original metal support, links traditional and modern architectural details in a workshop conversion. (Furniture designer/maker: Andrew Mortada.)

right Basic cabinets have been upgraded with gold leaf and varnish. They consist of a stack of two individual cabinets, with TV, video, and music equipment under lock and key, and children's toys below. (Design: Justin Meath Baker.)

below A sculptural music cabinet in beaten lead, aluminum, and wood provides storage for a bank of equipment, and adds a powerful presence in a modern environment. (Weymouth cupboard and CD cabinet by Malcolm Temple.)

Even in high-tech warehouse or loft conversions, on-view entertainment equipment can often look too raw and industrial. In a conventional house or apartment, managing this juxtaposition is a challenge. Yet entertainment equipment is now a key element in many living spaces, so aim to incorporate equipment in an accessible yet stylish way.

Function and decoration can be combined by using distinctive storage items to conceal bulky or incongruous pieces of equipment. Alternatively, customize an existing cabinet. Transform inexpensive composite or pine cabinets with silver or gold leaf and varnish or architectural molding. Use contrasting paint colors or cover them with burlap, string, or thin sheets of zinc or copper; change the existing pulls to cut-glass spheres or something organic like twigs or found driftwood. For modern eclectics, eccentric gothic-style hand-me-downs, antiquities, or anything ethnic will work well, especially in contrast to a modern backdrop. Likewise, contemporary pieces in a historic setting will look singular and impressive. Always try to give decorative storage items visual prominence and space.

above An Oriental-style set of drawers in composite and resin provides distinctive storage for everyday paperwork, videos, and CDs – in contrast to a sandblasted brick interior. (Furniture designer/maker: Andrew Mortada.)

left Ideal for concealing entertainment equipment, a traditional New England cabinet provides essential storage in historic style. In addition to this, a traditional blanket box doubles as both a table and as storage for books and magazines.

right A fork-lift device is in keeping with the size statement of the TV, video, and music system in this New York apartment. A basket for CDs and videos, with black-and-white prints on top, offsets this raw industrial style.

below Compact and mobile, a simple storage system with TV platform, video shelf, and box for tapes can be wheeled into position for viewing when needed. (Biblica from Arc Linea.)

If you enjoy watching TV and videos frequently, invest in a sizeable screen and position it for direct viewing. However, a television that sits directly in front of a sofa or in the center of general living space can conflict with alternative activities and encourage passive, automatic viewing.

Storing entertainment equipment on carts, mobile cabinets, or pivoting wall brackets and moving it into position when you want to use it gives you immediate access along with the flexibility to do something else without effort. Choose a style of storage to fit in with existing decoration – perhaps a lightweight aluminum cart with adjustable shelves, or a low wooden cabinet with a stacking device for TV and VCR and a drawer for video tapes. If you favor stark contrasts between high technology and domesticity, opt for heavy-duty fixtures designed for professional studios.

left Compact music systems on lightweight carts are ideal to move around single-level apartments. Beware of moving music systems with multiple cables. (Habitat.)

right This plastic basket is ideal for transporting CDs. Keep current favorites on view next to a music system for easy access, and store the bulk of a collection elsewhere. (Hold Everything.)

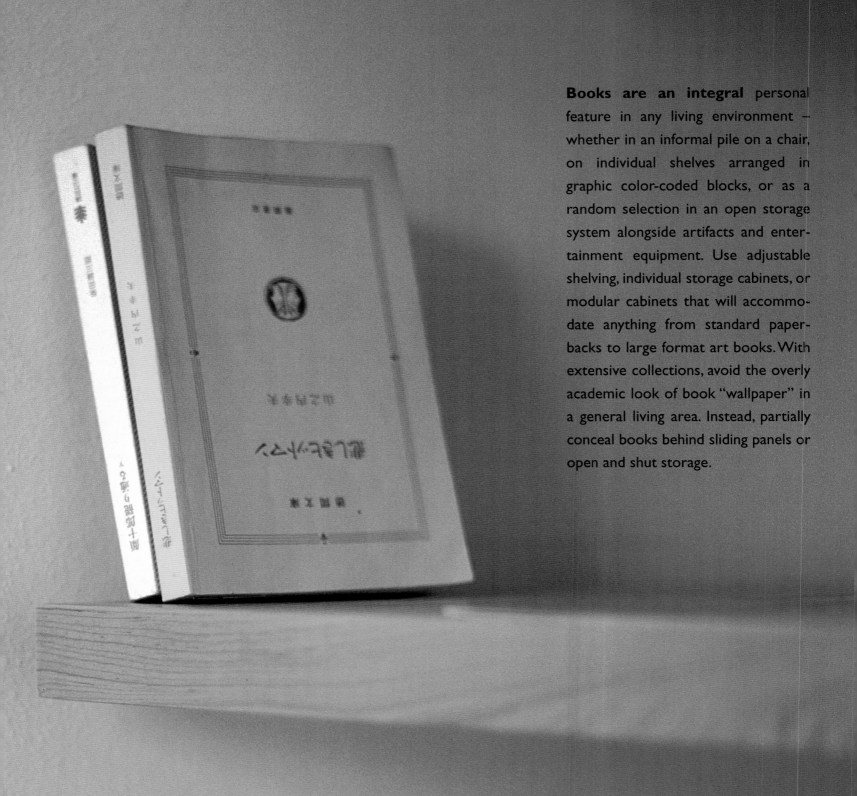

Books are an integral personal feature in any living environment – whether in an informal pile on a chair, on individual shelves arranged in graphic color-coded blocks, or as a random selection in an open storage system alongside artifacts and entertainment equipment. Use adjustable shelving, individual storage cabinets, or modular cabinets that will accommodate anything from standard paperbacks to large format art books. With extensive collections, avoid the overly academic look of book "wallpaper" in a general living area. Instead, partially conceal books behind sliding panels or open and shut storage.

books

above Modular units with open and shut storage can conceal a mass of books and bulky entertainment equipment, while revealing a decorative selection of books and artifacts.

left A bold wooden shelf across an odd space makes a useful and unobtrusive bookshelf. Beware of utilizing every spare bit of space for book storage and thus overpowering a general living area.

above A conventional yet practical storage solution: building a bookcase in an architectural alcove. Use vertical tracks with adjustable shelving for maximum flexibility.

right A country-style wall rack makes convenient storage for magazines, newspapers, and paperbacks. As alternative storage for a selection of books, use a basket or compact cart.

If you can designate space in general living areas for book storage and reading, celebrate with a distinctive storage item – perhaps a rotating book stand or a mobile cabinet with internal shelving; or construct a stack or spiral of inexpensive wooden boxes. Simply stand one on top of the other and let the weight of books act as anchor, or use screws to join them together top and bottom.

Open shelving or low cabinets double as convenient book storage and partitions within open-plan areas. Alternatively, to keep space free and flexible (especially in conventional setups), utilize outer-perimeter storage potential – floor-to-ceiling shelving systems in alcoves or comprehensive wall systems, for example. For a mass of books, store the collection in a shelving system with sliding front panels or doors in wood, metal, or semitransparent glass and reveal different sections at a time. For a similar partial-reveal effect, stretch blank canvas over a light frame and prop it up against conventional book shelves.

left In an open-plan New York apartment, welcoming chairs and a rotating bookstand define a light and spacious reading area.

below Low cabinets or mobile units such as this provide convenient book storage and can also be used as space dividers to create a quiet area for reading.

right A vast Indian bowl is an imaginative storage solution for reference books and magazines, and sits perfectly between home office and general living area.

For a mixture of books and artifacts in open storage, vertical tracks with adjustable shelves or modular building-block systems with various shelving options, provide flexible, no-fuss solutions.

Tracking systems give maximum flexibility, especially for large art or reference books. Alternatively, install adjustable shelving within a kit framework. Mount tracks on the back of the cabinet or side verticals. Use wood for the frame and either wood, metal, or glass for shelving. Depending on the size of the cabinet and load capacity of the shelving, insert a vertical panel or track approximately every 20 inches (50.8 cm). Paint the cabinet (and back wall), the same color as the rest of the room to throw books and artifacts into relief. Or decorate to emphasize the frame, not the shelf positions within. Perhaps use contrasting paint colors for frame and shelving or mount architraving or facing on the frame.

left Books and artifacts on open shelving provide a decorative display. Paint units the same color as the surrounding walls to offset ceramics and pieces of art.

right A contemporary version of a cinderblock and plank shelf construction is collapsible and extendable horizontally and vertically with aluminum connector brackets. (Design: Ali Tayar.)

bedroom

left A wall of built-in closets – with wallcovering and paneling to match the rest of the room – provides extensive invisible bedroom storage.

the closet

left An ornate metal frame with drapes makes decorative freestanding storage. As an alternative to metal, put together a simple wooden frame or box and hang plain canvas banners all around.

above This expandable flexible storage system – with basic steel frame, shelf, and clothes rod fronted by a curtain pole and cotton drapes – provides ample hanging and shelf space.

right A substantial storage solution that makes use of built-in closets on either side of a window. Natural Roman shades, instead of traditional doors, hide clothes and shoes.

Creating the right environment for sleep and relaxation is very important – so plan bedroom storage with special care and attention to detail. If space is at a premium and a bedroom is also an office, gym, or alternative television room, then organization and flexible storage are especially critical. The closet is usually the central storage item in the bedroom. A mixture of hanging and drawer or shelf space will provide all the basic storage requirements for clothing. Take into account the ratio of hanging space to shelf space available, together with the overall space and structure or architecture of the environment, to find a workable storage solution.

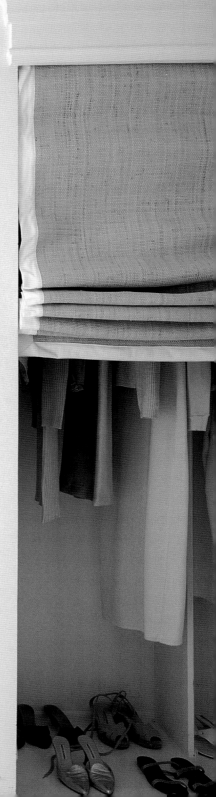

A single storage network of inexpensive self-assembly metal, composite board, or pine drawers with basic hanging rods and adjustable shelving systems can provide complete bedroom storage. Arrange the network along one wall or divide it between two alcoves. Contain everything in an overall framework and conceal with sliding panels, doors, or a curtain on a metal pole.

Individual storage sections can be concealed in different ways – for example, hang a linen shade in front of shelves, leave a section of baskets or storage boxes on view, and install a sliding mirror panel in front of clothes rods. In period-style interiors where the walls are decorated with paneling or wallpaper, match the closet fronts to the rest of the scheme, continue any architrave or baseboard, and create an invisible wall of storage.

Open storage for clothing is another option, and is ideal for minimalists or anyone who favors a strict color code. Avoid overloading open rails, or clashing colors and patterns – the effect can be chaotic. Clothing bags or canvas or plastic bags with front zippers will help reduce the jumbled effect and protect clothes from dust.

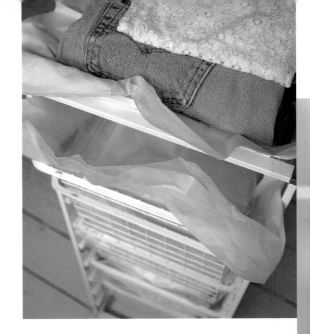

above A metal frame cabinet with deep drawers provides ample storage for underwear, sweaters, shirts, and jeans. Each drawer can be lined with tissue paper to help keep clothes pristine.

below Storing out-of-season sweaters and shirts in a transparent envelope will protect them from dust in a drawer or open shelf. Bags with canvas backing help clothes "breathe."

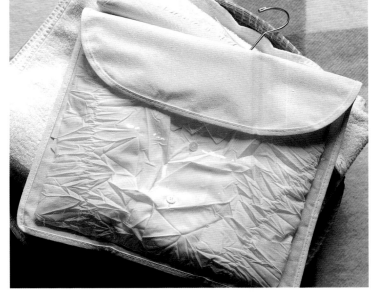

above As an original alternative to clothes rods running parallel to a wall, these head-on clear plastic rods provide compact storage.

right Functional and stylish open storage with clear plastic rods and sculptural shelf, inspired by Gabriella Ligenza's London hat shop fittings. Plastic boxes store special items on the top shelf. (Design: Janie Jackson.)

Choose high-quality fittings and fixtures such as sculptural shelves, plastic clothes rods, or metal structures for distinctive open bedroom storage. Supplement minimalist clothes rods with additional storage for everyday sweaters, shirts, and underwear; a simple line of open baskets, an independent set of drawers, or accessible shelves will work well. Cardboard or plastic boxes with lids, impractical for everyday use, are ideal for storing less frequently worn or out-of-season clothes.

Explore the possibility of installing compact sets of drawers, or shelves that will hold a line of boxes or baskets, within existing closets. Characterful period pieces such as armoires, with only a single rod or three or four shelves, can be imaginatively refitted to provide ample storage. Incorporate space-saving devices like a spinning tie-rack on a hook or hang shoe organizers or bags inside doors.

For any additional bedroom storage, offset period pieces with contemporary items such as a Plexiglas trolley with drawers. Be creative when mixing styles and sizes, and consider painting or silver-leafing dark wood pieces to lighten any grandiose effect.

left A compact tie spinner neatly stores ties. Utilize small-scale storage solutions like this to improve organization and protect clothing within traditional or contemporary closets.

right An architectural metal structure at one end of this bedroom provides hanging space for suit bags with cheap and cheerful brown paper bags below for underwear, sweaters, and T-shirts. (Design: Justin Meath Baker.)

below Moroccan-style drapes and a kilim transform a simple alcove closet into a striking feature. If possible, install a wall or ceiling light when partitioning walk-in storage space.

left Voluminous drawstring sacks with contrasting interlinings make jolly storage for toys. They are easy to carry from one play area to another and ideal for a quick toy sweep when play is over.

right and below An inventive twist on underbed storage: a bed that pulls out from and stores away underneath a magnificent glass display platform revealing a collection of sea treasures. The room has ample storage for clothing in lockers and hung from clothes rods. This is a compact and inventive design solution that downplays the bed as a dominant feature of the room without major disruption or effort. (Architectural design: Charles Rutherfoord.)

bed and
bedside

The style, size, and position of a bed is a key factor in organizing space and planning storage solutions in a sleeping environment. Flexible bedroom furniture, such as roll-up futons, beds that hinge or pivot out of the way, sofabeds, or bed platforms, can provide valuable extra storage space. But there are many alternative simple storage ideas, often centered under or beside the bed, that suit conventional arrangements and maximize the sense of space.

right Decorative chairs provide simple storage for everyday clothing and clean laundry. With ample storage elsewhere, witty details like this enliven an interior.

above An American chicken crate makes an inexpensive country-style low table and storage box. Do not restore simple crates and boxes, as you run the risk of taking away essential texture and character — simply remove dangerous nails or splinters and paint or stain.

right A cast-off display cabinet fits conveniently beneath a window to provide expansive storage space in the bedroom. The contents can be partly concealed by stapling muslin or linen over glass panels, or replacing clear glass with sand-blasted glass.

Many contemporary bed designs integrate storage space for essential items. Space for books and reading lamps can be found within headboards, swivel side tables, or vast mattress platforms with runaround, benchlike shelves. For a simple headboard and shelf combination, set a divan or bed base away from the wall, run two long shelves behind it extending on each side of the base, then insert a masonite panel between the bed base and shelves. Place one shelf level with the bed base and one just below the top of the panel. Paint everything one color and slide the bed base up against the panel. Use the top shelf for storing books or to prop up a favorite painting. Use the lower shelf, concealed behind the masonite panel, for storing infrequently used items.

As an alternative to traditional pieces such as blanket boxes, use wicker hampers or travel chests to store spare pillows and out-of-season comforters. Look out for quirky used display cabinets and line glass panels with muslin or gauze.

left An architectural recess shelf above this bed provides storage for bedside essentials, in addition to swivel side tables. Clothing is housed in a mobile closet with aluminum doors. (Furniture from Ligne Roset.)

Utilizing space under a bed for practical storage is worth every effort. Even if saving space is a not an issue, exploit the potential to store substantial amounts of clothing, bedding, or equipment conveniently out of sight.

Built-in drawers in bed frames can provide expansive underbed storage – ideal for shirts, sweaters, spare bed linen, and blankets. If space is tight and side drawers are inconvenient, put drawers at the foot of the bed for easier access.

As an alternative to built-in storage, combine any high-level bed with independent low-level storage. A wooden platform (or possibly even a single drawer from a pine chest) on heavy-duty castors provides a perfect base for storage. Either place items directly onto the platform, or store within open boxes or baskets on top of the platform.

Use boxes with lids to protect clothes from dust, and store sweaters and shirts in transparent clothes bags in open baskets or containers; use muslin drawstring liners and seal individual piles, or simply place a linen napkin or towel on top. For stability, anchor the containers to the platform or platforms with screws or glue.

above A custom-built bed with large underbed drawers for shirts, T-shirts, sweaters, and spare bed linen makes the most of otherwise "dead" space. Two distinctive bedside cabinets, one a practical cube design and one artistic and decorative, complete this idiosyncratic scheme. (Design: Justin Meath Baker.)

right A bed on a scaffolding frame sits high enough for easy underbed access. Canvas containers on wheels provide useful additional storage for clothing and blankets.

left Open canvas or cardboard boxes are ideal for underbed storage. To protect clothing from dust, use transparent plastic bags or containers.

bathroom

Include storage ideas at the planning stage of any new bath or shower room. A simple recess shelf in the wall of the shower area for gels and lotions is integral to the design and space in a way that a soap-on-a-rope hanging on a nozzle is not. If you plan to conceal pipework with a false wall, continue the false wall to the ceiling and create a recessed shelving system that you can either leave open or conceal with a sliding mirror panel or mirror doors.

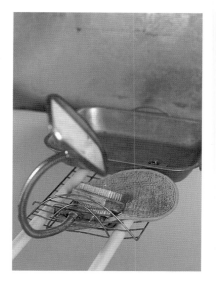

left This bath rack cleverly uses everyday items. A draining rack and roasting pan sit on plastic poles with a flexible rear-view mirror and provide no-fuss storage for a daily shave. (Design: Justin Meath Baker.)

towels and
toiletries

left This metal basket allows a bar of soap to drain and sits at an angle for easy access. As long as soap is not swimming in a puddle of water, any small pot, bowl, or basket will work well.

left A perfect compact arrangement for people who get soap in their eyes. Everything is conveniently on hand, from underbasin cabinet to toothbrush rack and linen bag — all in period style.

above Concealing hot and cold water pipes and the toilet cistern behind wood paneling provides a useful run-around shelf for bowls, boxes, mirror, and bathroom cabinet.

Standing at a basin to wash requires immediate access to essential items in a compact space – from soap, nailbrush, and toothbrush to washcloths and towels. The advantage of basins with built-in surrounds—anything from an architectural piece of glass or slab of stone to a traditional washstand with a basin set into wood or marble—is that essential items are all within easy reach. The main disadvantage is that excessive splashing will soak everything.

To keep soap or wooden brushes from sitting in a puddle of water, store them in a wire basket or use traditional marble dishes with drainage holes. Drain toothbrushes by standing them in a metal or glass tumbler. For an ad hoc solution, use a sculptural stainless steel colander and store everything together. It is a pity to use only specialist bathroom fixtures like chrome toothbrush holders or soap dishes on wall brackets when often a favorite bowl or something basic from the kitchen will provide effective storage with originality.

right A sculptural basin and surround present an imaginative storage solution for soaps and lotions. Glass shelves above the bathtub provide backup storage for additional items. (Architects: Munkenbeck + Marshall.)

left In this compact bathroom, simple storage items include basic soap dish, mirror cabinet, and shelf. Towels and clothing hang on a heated towel rod beside the door. Architects: (Munkenbeck + Marshall.)

right Hanging cylindrical canvas sacks provide useful additional storage on the back of a door. Simply thread plastic-coated garden wire through drawstring bags, make a wire loop at one end, and hang on simple hooks.

Shelves and cabinets above basins provide practical eye-level storage. Do not limit yourself to bathroom-specific versions. Consider stainless steel racks from kitchen suppliers, wood and metal food lockers, or simple open shelf systems, and use as inexpensive alternatives to standard metal or wood mirrored-door cabinets. Hang a plain mirror above a basin with shelf brackets on each side, and use driftwood, slate, or copper sheeting for inexpensive individual shelving.

If a basin stands in front of a window, use the windowsill or install a single shelf below the window frame. As an alternative, stretch high-tension wire across the window frame, using eye plates and a wire tensioner (from sports equipment suppliers), and hook up a mirror and wire basket for toothbrushes, soap, and washcloths.

A cabinet under a basin is a very logical use of space. It can conceal pipework and provides ample hideaway storage. Use it to store special items, backup supplies, and cleaning materials.

left Japanese bathing principles in a workshop conversion include cedar bath and separate shower for washing hidden behind a mosaic panel. A simple set of drawers and wall of cabinets store towels and cleaning materials.

Part of the pleasure of getting in a bathtub is not getting out again until you choose to. Store essentials and lotions within easy reach of the tub. The simplest storage solution is a rack that fits across the tub or a series of metal baskets that hang over the side. An inexpensive basket or bucket hanging on a faucet will work just as well.

If you plan to enclose a bathtub, aim to incorporate a wide storage shelf – ideally all around the tub or, if space is tight, on one side or one end. If the bathtub is set against a wall, insert a series of hooks along the wall just above the level of the bath and store supplies in a row of small baskets. A folding chair can provide temporary storage beside the bath.

Shower enclosures require no-fuss storage solutions. Plan any storage at the design stage if possible and incorporate an alcove in the wet area for shower gels and shampoo, and a dry area for towels and clothing. For example, a shelf above the shower head or, in a compact space, a plastic box with a lid will keep essentials dry. In simple enclosures, shower racks hanging on a hook or over a temperature control switch will store gels, soap, and brushes within easy reach.

right Incorporate storage ideas at the planning stage of a new bathroom, like this colorful tongue-and-groove plan with built-in bath and shelf surround and recess with glass shelves. (Design: Justin Meath Baker.)

below Simple metal loops for towels, clothes, and bathrobe augment a traditional kitchen chair for practical storage. On bathtubs with sloping sides, a run-around rod is ideal for hanging bath towels. (Design: Philippe Starck for Duravit.)

right Internal shelves in a deep curving bathroom door create inventive storage boxes for toiletries, books, and loofahs. As an alternative, hang a line of bicycle baskets or plastic containers down the middle of a plain door for easy access. A round basin cabinet provides contrasting hideaway storage. (Design: Justin Meath Baker.)

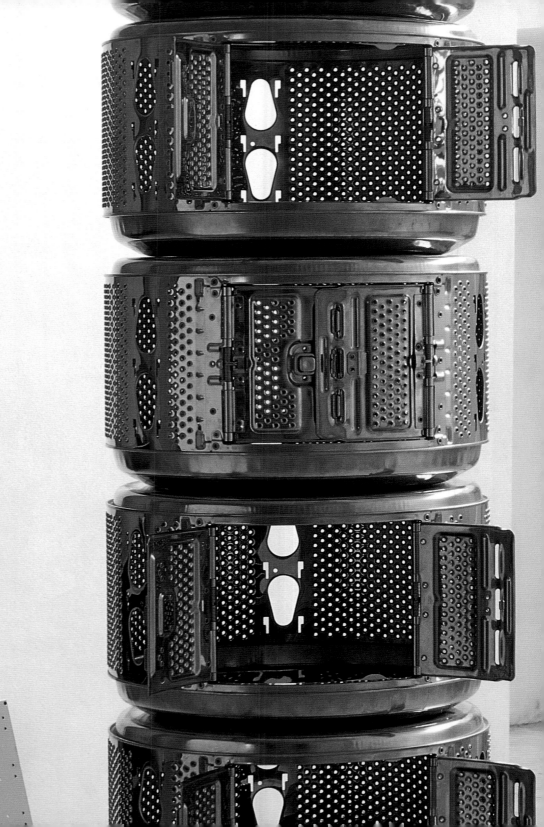

kitchen

ergonomics

With resourceful planning it is possible to design an informal, user-friendly kitchen with a minimum of fuss and expense. Begin with a review of basic appliances and storage requirements. Draw a map or plan of your existing kitchen, plot any changes or additions on paper, and re-use or reorganize anything you can. A few simple adjustments can make all the difference to day-to-day efficiency and practicality.

above Hanging wall cabinets are the main feature of this food preparation area. Pull-out box drawers house pans and utensils. (Design: Rick Baker.)

below A contemporary stainless steel rail in this Japanese kitchen echoes the style of a traditional American Shaker design and provides good eye-level storage.

above Making the most of available light and space under a roof, everything is close at hand in this kitchen. Cabinets pull out to provide extra surfaces for food preparation. (Design: Justin Meath Baker.)

above Inexpensive zinc sheets held in place with glue and upholstery tacks transform basic cabinets. Bright paintwork inside the cabinets, and hand-crafted pulls complete an inspiring make-over. (Design: Justin Meath Baker.)

right In this New York loft, open shelving holds pans, china, and glassware, while a row of cabinets underneath provides good-looking storage for kitchen basics. Specialist utensils and equipment are stacked neatly under walk-around tables.

A new relaxation about food preparation, a preference for sharing informal meals in the kitchen with family and friends, and a demand for simple environments signal a change in kitchen design and storage style. This keep-it-simple approach adapts easily to any style. So work within an existing architectural framework, apply simple ergonomics, and update any kitchen to a functional and welcoming space.

Before you go ahead with a major reorganization, run a quick check on all equipment, utensils, and tableware. Divide everything into essential items for accessible storage and nonessential items. Use this opportunity to remove any duplicates or extinct items. Why keep identical cheese graters or a rusty wok? Be realistic about storage options. Set a budget and invest in workable solutions that fit all individual requirements. There is no point buying an expensive, good-looking system with inadequate storage space. Also, it is important to avoid overcrowding – for safety reasons and for efficiency.

left In this dynamic conversion of a 19th-century workshop, a steel bar full of hanging pans and utensils means that all essential cooking items are close at hand.

For an efficient kitchen, begin with the position of basic appliances. Provide storage for cookware and tableware within an arm's span of key work stations and activity areas — so, store pots and pans next to a cooking appliance and knives and chopping board next to a work surface. Store tableware next to a sink, dishwasher, or table.

Storage possibilities are limitless, ranging from an informal combination of freestanding furniture, open shelving, and hanging racks to a system of built-in cabinets. The key factor in choosing effort-saving solutions is proximity. A drawer under a cooking appliance for pots and pans, pull-out baskets for food storage next to a work surface, or a wall rack beside a sink for clean china and glassware, all provide simple storage and upgrade kitchen efficiency. In a one-wall line-up with all appliances and storage together, the big issue is space-saving flexible storage. Compact options include pull-out shelf racks for food, deep drawers for cookware and tableware, a hanging rack for pots and pans, and a wheel-out cabinet or trolley with work surface and shelves underneath. Any remaining space is free for a table and chairs and general living space.

above A wooden wall slides across to enclose a kitchen, leaving the refrigerator/freezer in the dining area. Behind panels, this appliance is unobtrusive in an open-plan setting. (Architects: Munkenbeck + Marshall.)

left Plain, functional, and well put together, this kitchen in an open-plan New York apartment illustrates the fine art of low-key storage.

right Basic white cabinets provide floor-level storage, practical for heavy items such as cleaning equipment and saucepans, as well as creating a strong base for a joint counter and kitchen table.

on **display**

Matter-of-fact storage solutions – from rustic baskets and mason jars to on-view collections of utensils or everyday foodstuffs – can add vitality and color to functional catering environments. Simple details such as a line of cooking oils or preserves on a stainless steel shelf or a stack of favorite mixing bowls on a plain counter will enliven any space. Open kitchen storage, with everyday items within easy reach, is perfect for busy cooks.

left In this compact country kitchen, a simple shelf, plastic plate rack, and swivel dish towel rod allows easy access.

below Crisscross stainless steel shelves with open brackets take up less visual space than conventional wooden versions. (Shelves from Slingsby.)

above Economy of effort is often a result of having essential utensils close at hand. This rustic flatware box is perfect for the middle of the table for everyday meals.

right An attractive raised-pattern tray carries espresso cups to the dining table and also acts as a portable makeshift draining board when it is lined with paper towels.

A kitchen with its workings and contents on view is a welcoming place and, crucially, everything is highly accessible.

Typical storage solutions include basic utensils in ceramic pots; various rush baskets full of fresh vegetables, fruit, and eggs; jars of preserves displayed on shelves; and orderly stacks of cooking pots and bowls on a workbench or table. Perhaps as a backlash to laboratory-type kitchens, this tradition of presenting a visual index of essentials and things in store is back in favor. In moderation, and with twists to update this look, open storage translates well to even the most minimalist of kitchens.

Simplicity is the key. Avoid the confusion and chaos of taking everything you have out of the pantry and into the open. Instead, include only essential items in frequent use. Bear in mind that accessibility is as crucial as the visual effect. There is little point storing mason jars three-deep on a shelf, or putting your favorite salad bowl under a stack of heavy cookware so that it is difficult to remove.

left An out-of-service Dualit toaster is given shelf space as a rack for saucepan lids, while a galvanized bucket from a hardware store acts as a practical and generous utensil container.

An "open" kitchen can present many opportunities for creative storage ideas. Kitchen utensils can be stored in tool boxes, or even something as basic as a tin bucket or a terra-cotta plant pot. By pooling together odds and ends, clutter can be eliminated. A white pitcher with a selection of favorite wooden implements or an Oriental basket or steamer holding a jumble of cooking oils, spice jars, and herbs looks efficient and hardworking if placed next to the stove.

Kitchens with an emphasis on display are convenient for busy cooks who need to have everything at hand. For unusual ad hoc storage solutions, choose whatever items fit the environment. A sudden contrast—perhaps an African basket in a marble and stainless-steel kitchen—will look over-exotic. In general, resourceful yet compatible storage works best: Provençal storage jars and creamware pitchers for rustics, white ceramics and maple baskets for purists, and metal beakers or glass tank vases for modernists.

left Good accessibility is the feature of this kitchen storage solution. Equipment for food preparation or cooking is neatly stacked and clearly in view. This is no-fuss storage for people who like to cook.

left An orderly line of stainless steel and glass jars in different sizes provides convenient storage for everyday essentials including coffee and sugar.

below A foldaway two-tier plate rack in stainless steel and wood helps to drain and store china, glasses, and flatware.

left Individual lift-out containers inside kitchen drawers separate different types of utensils and prevent the usual jumble of everything thrown together.

below A mobile work surface with wide drawer, towel rods, and adjustable shelves is ideal for wheeling into action when needed, then storing out of the way.

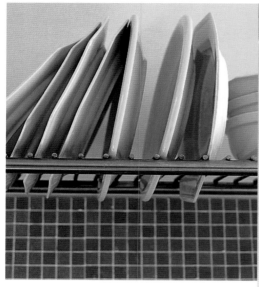

above A stainless steel rack above a work surface. With a mosaic tile area below, it is ideal for draining as well as storing plates.

below Stainless steel bars give this modern kitchen a professional catering look: convenient for drainage, quick access, and for hooking up pots and pans.

left This is functional yet decorative storage. Secure a firm anchor for butcher's hooks in an exposed beam or wooden rod and hook up kitchen utensils and earthenware pots.

right A series of parallel steel rods fitted with hooks provide compact storage for pans, skillets, and utensils. (Architects: Solveig Fernlund & Neil Logan.)

lofty
ideas

A simple hook can have a big impact upon the efficiency of a kitchen – in a way that expensive storage solutions and kitchen designs often do not. Everyday utensils and pans hanging within easy reach of a cooking surface symbolize a cook at work. Hooks and hanging rods provide logical and functional no-fuss storage for working kitchens.

Hooks and hanging rods, with a jumble of pans and utensils, offer an anti-order storage option. There are no cabinet doors to open or slide out of the way, and no place for artifice or to display items that collect dust—just sensible storage for everyday equipment

Before you opt for this level of exposure, lay out everything you plan to hang up. Divide up and position items according to function in the kitchen; for example, place cups by the coffee maker and pans and utensils by the stove. Take a look at how much there is to hang (allow for a few acquisitions over time) and figure out where everything can go.

Use hooks, hanging rods, or frames. Simple hooks work well for small items such as earthenware pitchers or aprons and dishtowels. Rods and frames are ideal for pans and utensils. Good anchorage to a wall or beam is critical, especially if you plan to hang everything with a handle from a single steel rod. Hanging frames, perhaps above a work surface, will distribute weight evenly.

left A luggage rack from a train provides versatile storage for kitchen utensils. With scope to hook up baskets for added small-scale storage, it makes a striking display.

left A washing machine, drier, refrigerator, freezer, and set of pull-out food racks form a precise geometric arrangement in this kitchen. Swing-open doors provide easy access to laundry appliances and conceal control panels. (Architect: Gunnar Orefelt.)

right Opaque Plexiglas panels create a seamless line from standard kitchen cabinets and basic appliances. A continuous counter and mosaic splashback complete the architectural simplicity of the scheme. (Architects: Munkenbeck + Marshall.)

below A spacious drawer underneath an oven and range provides ample storage for roasting pans, baking sheets, and large chopping boards. The wood-veneer finish on the drawer coordinates with kitchen cabinets throughout.

appliances

Raw kitchen appliances can look out of place within a coordinating kitchen, so storage is a critical factor. Replace or install fascia panels on appliance doors to conceal standard fixtures and unify a design scheme. Store laundry appliances in a separate area, or fit them into standard kitchen cabinet frames with swing-open doors to reduce noise levels and hide control panels. Check ventilation and plumbing requirements before committing to any changes.

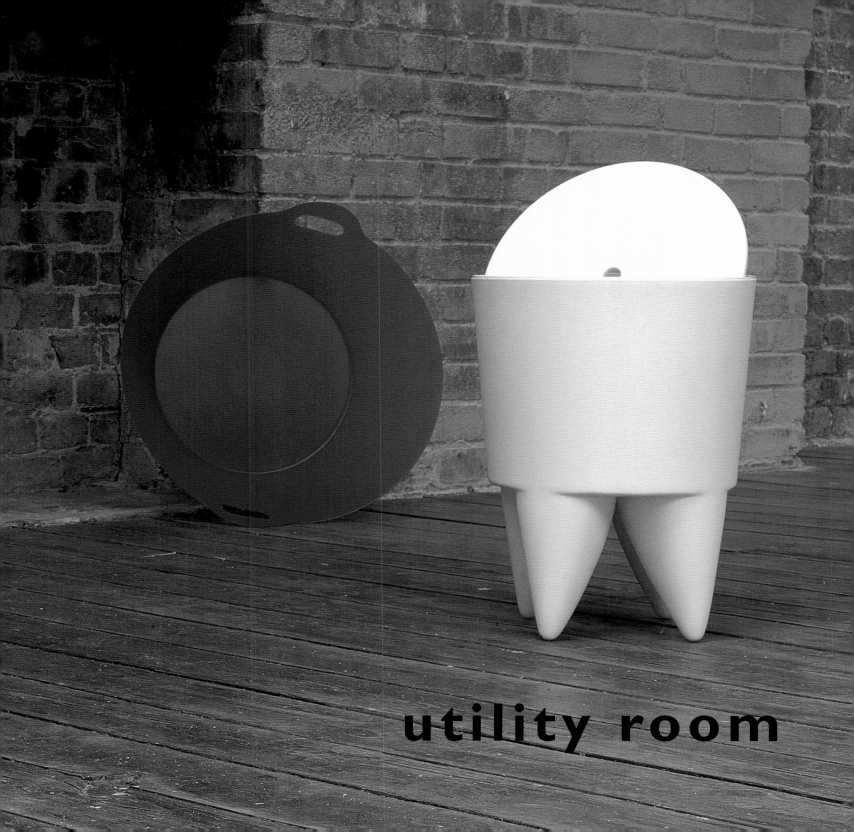

utility room

right This compact canvas and metal frame laundry basket for bathrooms and bedrooms is a welcome update on conventional Alibaba baskets.

left The luxury and convenience of a traditional built-in storage cupboard is shown off in this London townhouse. Narrow shelves inside provide ample storage space for bed linen, towels, and essential supplies. (Design: Eliza Cairns.)

cleaning and
laundry

Without labor-saving ideas and good storage solutions, cleaning and laundry can be a real chore. Simple ideas, such as storing laundry detergent on a shelf above a washing machine and sorting cleaning equipment into individual buckets for particular cleaning tasks, can minimize effort. Flexible options such as folding laundry carts and pull-up ceiling racks provide instant storage. Likewise, pull-out and wheel-around kitchen cabinets with shelves for cleaning equipment or an ironing board on a permanent pull-down wall installation, provide flexible storage to increase efficiency and convenience.

above In this compact utility area, all the essentials are stored within easy reach. Restaurant canisters hold detergents and related items, while buckets are housed under the sink.

right Wheel out this professional metal container on washdays for storing substantial laundry bundles. It is also useful for transporting cleaning equipment. (From Slingsby.)

above This foldaway lightweight laundry cart with removable stringmesh bag and wheels is ideal for collecting and storing wash or general household items. (From Slingsby.)

right A sculptural shopping cart is perfectly compatible with the sandblasted glass partitions and industrial fixtures in this schoolhouse conversion. Its graphic profile compensates for its basic function of storing bathroom supplies.

below Once a clothing locker at a New York public swimming pool, this wire basket is convenient for storing spare candles and specialized cleaning equipment for silverware. Use any wicker basket or container in this way.

right The front of this mobile kitchen cabinet flips down to reveal a plastic trash can. Inside, a network of different shelves provide specific storage for cleaning rags and food storage bags. (Design: Justin Meath Baker.)

For the storage of large-scale cleaning and laundry equipment, like vacuum cleaners and ironing boards, decide on a single cabinet if you can, and keep everything in one place for convenience. Arrange equipment so that heavy items are directly on the floor and nearest the door to save unnecessary lifting. For cleaning equipment with long tubing, remove the plastic hose and hang it over a nail or hook. Brooms and mops can be hung on the inside of the door. Buy the sort that have a handle with a hole in the top, or drill a hole in the top and thread a loop of string or tape to hook onto hardware on the wall.

Buckets provide perfect storage for cleaning rags, liquid sprays, and polish. Store everything in one bucket and simply take it with you on your chores. In addition to being portable, buckets can hang out of the way or stack on top of each other to save space. Pick up laundry in mobile foldaway containers, or line conventional laundry baskets with laundry bags and simply remove the bag full of laundry on washdays.

right An inexpensive plastic container with handle is handy for heavy-duty cleaning. Replace the lid for practical permanent storage for rags, trash can liners, and liquid sprays.

home office

right Multi-drawer units such as this wire system provide storage for essential office items. Invent a quick-search system by attaching photographs of what is inside on the front of each drawer.

left Good-sized baskets in metal make ideal portable storage containers for paperwork or files. Look out for ex-industrial metal trays in office warehouse sales or seek out exotic grocery boxes.

pen and
paper

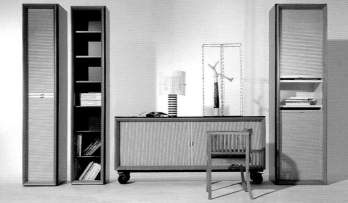

right A Mexican table, sculptural metal stools, an original clothes locker from a public swimming pool, and metal jars for pens and pencils provide stylish basics for a daytime office area at one end of this New York apartment. (Design: C.I.T.E.)

below Library and department-store style are combined in these traditional storage items. Such pieces do not look out of place in modern home offices.

above Precision building-block units for equipment and information storage coordinate to individual specifications to provide flexible add-on home office storage.

right In any office in a home environment, special human elements, like this collection of Oriental baskets for storing pencils and elastic bands, will serve to offset worklike precision and conformity.

Working from home is now a viable empowering option for many people. The rapid expansion in communication networks, inexpensive computer systems, and new thinking about how, where, and when we work all contribute to this change. Yet setting up an office at home can create unique problems. Organization with flexibility and imaginative storage is the key to success in any environment.

If you opt to work from home, aim to take over a whole room and set it up as a welcoming, ready-to-use environment. There is no reason for this space to look like a conventional office, and as it is self-contained you will not be restricted to fitting in with design decisions elsewhere in the house. However, it is possible that you will have to use an area within an established room for your home office. The main consideration with dual-function environments is how to organize space and store equipment without compromising work or living activities.

Apart from essential investments such as excellent seating, a solid work surface, good basic equipment, and lighting, this is an ideal opportunity to invest in creative storage solutions. Mix industrial shelving with metal cupboards and mobile sets of drawers in low-key industrial style; perhaps opt for a traditional oak desk with library shelves and consider commissioning a custom-built system of storage cabinets and work surface or choose specialized items from contract suppliers.

right In a New York apartment, a modernist red table effectively frames and diffuses the raw industrial feel of an assertive line-up of heavy-duty metal filing cabinets. (Design: C.I.T.E.)

Whether your idea of an essential work space is a computer terminal with fax, answering machine, and coffee maker, or a plain table with a sheet of paper and a pencil, ample storage will prevent an office from taking over a domestic set-up.

Open-plan interiors offer many possibilities for delineating office space. Partitions or storage units can divide working and living areas. For conventional dual-function areas (a kitchen table, bedroom alcove, or hallway), reorganize existing storage or introduce mobile storage cabinets. Alternatively, choose new cabinets with ample storage potential in a style that is in keeping with existing surroundings. A metal front-opening travel trunk, an Indian temple cupboard, Shaker-style kitchen cabinet, or modular wall units all provide functional options and fit in with contemporary interiors. For fax machines, small printers, and photocopiers, sturdy trolleys in metal, plastic, or wood are the best option. The simpler the storage solution, the quicker the transition from work space to living space, and vice versa.

above In an open-plan New York apartment, an antique desk and modern plastic trolley provide ample storage and work space.

left Good organization and under-desk storage limits the impact of essential computer equipment and office paperwork upon living space.

right Mobile storage cabinets can wheel in and out to screen office activities during working hours. (Mobile unit from Driade.)

right Built in a prime position in good light, this flip-down desk makes clever use of space. Cabinets below and on each side provide storage for books, files, and a fax machine.

small-scale storage

small-scale
storage

Finding storage solutions for small-scale essentials will revolutionize the way you live with a new sense of order. Avoid convention and use kitchen items in bathrooms for storing sponges, soaps, and body brushes; introduce office surplus into bedrooms for socks, underwear, and accessories; and bring plant pots into kitchens to store stainless steel and wooden utensils. As well as providing decorative and personal storage, explore the hidden possibilities of plastic boxes as drawer dividers and baskets inside cabinets for extra efficiency and a welcome sense of space.

above A simple metal basket makes a convenient organizer for kitchen sink clutter, such as washing brushes, cloths, and liquids. Use a separate basket for storing clean cutlery or vegetable brushes.

right Any size or shape of rustic basket provides ideal storage in a country-style interior. Hang them from simple nails or hooks in kitchens, bathrooms, or hallways for household essentials.

left Inexpensive Oriental baskets, like this Chinese vegetable steamer (available from specialized supermarkets or kitchen suppliers), can be easily upgraded to become decorative storage items.

above Store everyday kitchen utensils in simple open baskets for order and accessibility. Teaspoons can be placed alongside a kettle, while cooking oils and utensils can sit next to a cooking surface.

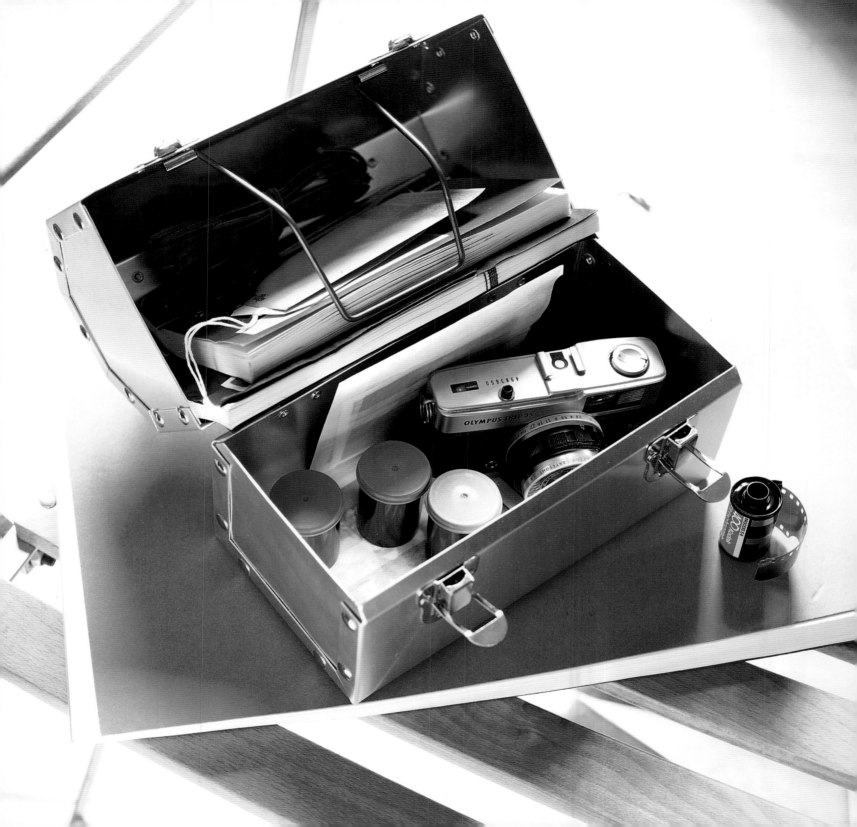

left Sweep up any random collections of vacation photographs, household bills and documents, or CDs in multi-use cardboard and metal storage boxes. They are ideal for visible stacks on tables or on open shelving systems, inside closets or under beds. (Boxes from Muji.)

right Pull-out boxes for sewing kits or baskets for knitting provide lightweight portable storage. Use containers with pulls and devise an easy-reference labeling system — perhaps plastic bags stuck to the front with a sample of the contents.

left Metal or plastic lunch boxes make versatile and protective storage for special interest items such as camera equipment or art materials. For alternative hard-wearing storage containers, check office suppliers for petty-cash boxes, mini-safes, and filing boxes.

Boxes eliminate the visual clutter of collections of small-scale items and provide efficient storage solutions for everyday requirements, from a stack of CDs to household documents. Use plastic or cardboard open boxes for organizing the inside of cabinets; ideal for piles of T-shirts, table linen, or toys. Store boxes along the bottom of a cabinet or on basic shelving for easy access. For dust-free storage of fragile clothing, computer disks, or any paraphernalia not in everyday circulation, use boxes with lids.

As a low-cost do-it-yourself storage system, mount a series of parallel shelves on the wall to provide a basic framework. Then fill in rows of boxes. Install optional side panels for extra definition or even construct a free-standing frame on wheels. Either way, keep the top shelf clear for opening and sorting individual boxes. Design a quick-reference labeling system, perhaps luggage tags, colored adhesive labels, letters of the alphabet, or numbers. As an alternative, you can use a selection of semitransparent plastic boxes so you can see the individual contents at a glance.

Although there is a wide selection of specialty products and designs to match small-scale storage requirements for bathrooms, it is worth looking beyond the conventional choices and putting together an eclectic mixture of essentials with wit and originality.

Stick to basics if you want a contemporary style. Plain white china mugs, bowls, glass tumblers, and metal beakers provide low-cost storage for toothbrushes, natural sponges, and soaps. Often, a simple change of environment for familiar household objects is enough to create a new look.

Cosmetics and cotton balls can be stored in transparent pencil cases, food jars with snap-lids, and even in plastic food boxes. Use glass flower vases for body brushes and loofahs and frosty dessert dishes for soaps. Convert bubble-glass cooking oil jars and miniature spice jars into decorative storage for lotions and homemade aromatic bath oils.

left Simple white china, glass, and metal containers from the kitchen transfer to bathrooms for simple storage. Add a favorite decorative piece to enliven and personalize a basic lineup.

right Bring decorative garden urns and plant pots indoors for imaginative storage solutions. Also, mix together wire boxes, plant containers, and stone pots.

above Inexpensive terra-cotta pots and earthenware storage jars work well with period fittings and add color and texture to country-style bathrooms.

right Empty jelly jars or mason jars with snap-lids provide inexpensive solutions for keeping together essential odds and ends such as pencils, rubber bands, stamps, and paper clips.

Reinvent, recycle, and reuse familiar household items as alternative storage solutions. For example, transfer talcum powder to a sugar shaker for easy sprinkling, keep household receipts, take-out menus, and timetables on an office-surplus clipboard and hang it up on the back of a cabinet door; or reuse cardboard shoe boxes for photographs or stationery supplies.

Recycle jelly jars, plastic food containers, and cookie tins for convenient airtight food storage. Hardware stores and office suppliers are a good source for a mass of ad hoc storage items. Use expandable toolboxes for toiletries, cosmetics, or a sewing kit, or convert plastic mini drawer-systems, originally for screws and nails, for cotton swabs, tweezers, and nail scissors. Also, colorful petty-cash boxes or safes are ideal as jewelry boxes; metal or plastic paper trays work well as storage for belts and scarves, and wastepaper baskets are useful for keeping magazines and newspapers orderly in living environments.

right For low-cost storage, recycle food cans for pens and pencils, fabric swatches, or darning thread. Use a can opener to remove any sharp edges and wash the can thoroughly.

below Stacks of colorful rustic boxes provide decorative storage in both country-style and contemporary interiors.

right The simplicity and honesty of Shaker boxes can offset machine-age entertainment equipment in multi-functional living environments.

left Mix and match a collection of ethnic baskets for decorative color-coded storage on open shelving.

right A used swimsuit mannequin is an unusual hanging frame for kitchen mugs. Explore the possibilities of topiary frames in sculptural or animal shapes for a similar decorative display.

Transposing historic or ethnic storage items into contemporary settings can provide new storage possibilities far away from the original commonplace use.

Historic Shaker boxes, made by craftspeople for storing everyday kitchen and workshop items, now look out of place in workaday situations. Antique country boxes, earthenware or stone storage jars, milk pitchers, and medicine jars, once seen as functional items, are too precious for kitchen or household items. Use these storage treasures for jewelry, mementos, and anything of personal value. For decorative general storage, look to ethnic basketware and simple wooden boxes. Often inexpensive yet with fine detailing or craftwork, they are ideal for many practical storage applications. Use colorful African market baskets, originally used for carrying fruit and vegetables, to store clothing and magazines, and Oriental vegetable steamers or sisal spice baskets for cosmetics and toiletries.

Viewed with imagination, many antique items that were not originally designed for the purpose can also provide decorative storage. For example, antique hats can hold cosmetics, scarves, and belts.

yard and garage

storage
shelters

Garden sheds and garages require common-sense storage solutions. Gardening is a hands-on outdoor activity that begins with a visit to a shed, or possibly a shelf, to pick up your equipment. Apart from a table or counter for repotting or sharpening tools, a single row of long nails will provide no-fuss storage for hanging spades, rakes, and forks. A galvanized trash can will prevent fertilizers and plant food from drying out or getting too damp. In sizeable yards, a wheelbarrow is useful for transporting equipment, while a gardening apron with pockets is handy for compact tools.

above An outdoor peg rail under the shelter of an overhanging roof makes orderly storage for gardening tools, plant box, and wicker basket. A line of nails will work as well.

left A slatted wooden shelf on bracket mounts makes a simple, well-drained potting table with space to store various plants and galvanized florist's buckets.

left A traditional wicker gardener's basket sports sturdy handle and straps to hold tools and gardening gloves in place. With space for plants, seeds, or bulbs, it is a practical companion for any gardener.

left A rustproof galvanized can provides effective outdoor storage for a compact town garden. With room for a watering can, garden tools, fertilizers, and string, it is full without being chaotic or unworkable.

In garages, even with a car inside, there is ample storage potential on walls and ceilings. For sports equipment such as skis or bicycles, invest in specialized wall or ceiling brackets available from sports suppliers. Alternatively, for a bicycle, secure firm hardware for two heavy-duty shelf brackets and support the frame under the crossbar or below the seat and handle bars. For rackets, bats, balls, and sports shoes, put up a high-level shelf – a wooden rack on brackets or a series of wooden or metal parallel poles stretching across one wall with occasional brackets underneath for extra support. Hang hooks on the poles for additional storage of gardening implements or sports clothing.

For tools and household maintenance and decorating equipment, metal filing cabinets with good-sized drawers for cans of paint and electrical tools are in keeping with the workaday look of a garage environment. Plastic boxes and blockboard shelves or self-assembly cabinets work well for a mix of different tools, cans, and essentials.

left A self-assembly modular cabinet, with optional doors and shelf components, stores tools and equipment and provides a strong base for a work table. (From Cubestore.)

above Former household or broken items often resurface in tool sheds or garages as ad hoc storage solutions. This split flatware tray, in use as a catchall for paint brushes and varnish, is a typical example.

right Colorful plastic bottle crates brighten up a garage, cellar, modern kitchen, or understair area. Ideal for wine, water, or soft drinks, they can be stacked to save space. (Jasper Morrison rack.)

above For household maintenance or professional cleaning, this mobile unit offers a trash can and plastic vest for equipment. (From Slingsby.)